John Townsend

The Doom of Slavery in the Union

its safety out of it - Volume II

John Townsend

The Doom of Slavery in the Union
its safety out of it - Volume II

ISBN/EAN: 9783744731393

Printed in Europe, USA, Canada, Australia, Japan

Cover: Foto ©Suzi / pixelio.de

More available books at **www.hansebooks.com**

THE

DOOM OF SLAVERY

IN THE UNION:

ITS SAFETY

OUT OF IT.

SECOND EDITION.

☞ Read and Send to your Neighbor. ☜

CHARLESTON, S. C.
PRINTED BY EVANS & COGSWELL,
No. 3 Broad and 103 East Bay Streets.
1860.

ADDRESS

OF THE

HON. JOHN TOWNSEND.

The Edisto Island Vigilant Association being in session on Monday, October 29, the President, Hon. JOHN TOWNSEND, delivered the following address, which was ordered to be published :

GENTLEMEN OF THE ASSOCIATION : As we are organized for the object, especially, of protecting our slave institutions, it is proper that we should hold frequent counsel together, and carefully consider the modes by which it might be assailed.

The crisis is fast approaching, and a few brief weeks will decide whether we are to drag out a few years more of dishonored existence, under a Black Republican rule, which has openly declared their purpose to destroy us—or whether, casting all unmanly fears to the winds, we shall take our destiny under our own control, and with God to help us, resolve that we will be ruled only by ourselves.

From all present indications, Lincoln will be elected by the Electoral College ; but if not by that mode, then by Congress afterwards. With the whole North thoroughly sectionalized and given over to Abolitionism (a very small and uninfluential party only excepted), every Douglas Democrat, and every Bell and Everett supporter, in all that populous region, may be classed, as between Breckinridge and Lincoln, a supporter of the latter. In opinions and feelings they affiliate with the party which support him, as against the South ; and when the day of trial shall come, when they shall be required to indicate their preference, it will be found that they will be governed by their Abolition proclivities, and give their support in Congress to the nominee of the Black Republicans. The *principles*, then, of that dangerous party may be considered as those which are to control the Government after the 4th March next.

I know there is, with some, a feeble hope entertained that, if the election goes into Congress, Breckinridge, or Bell, or Lane, by some skillful management or good luck, might be slipped into the Presidency instead of Lincoln. But this hope, feeble as it is, must be regarded as a mere delusion ; or more probably, it is the resort of the timid, to postpone, and afterwards avoid, timely and manly resistance. But admitting it might be so, let it be considered that Mr. Buchanan with all his high claims to enlarged statesmanship, and with all his skill as an experienced politician, has been unable to conduct the Government upon the principles of justice and equality which the Constitution contemplates. Nor has he been able to protect even himself, as the Chief of the Executive Department of the Government, from the rude and aggressive assaults of the overbearing and irresponsible Black Republican majority, which has, now, control of the House of Representatives, and will soon have control of the Senate of the United States. How vain, then, and fallacious, is it to expect that either of the distinguished individuals above named (Breckinridge, Lane or Bell) will be able to accomplish what Mr. Buchanan has failed to achieve.

No President can protect the South.

We cannot, then, too soon realize to ourselves the impressive fact that, constituted as the Government of the United States now is, of two hostile parties, in which the Black Republicans have an overwhelming majority in the House of Representatives, as they will soon have in the Senate—a President becomes *powerless* to enforce the just obligations of each under the Constitution; and that he, as well as every other interest in the country, must expect to be brought under subjection to that ravening majority. In this view of the subject, how futile is it in the people of the South to place their dependence upon a President for their protection, no matter how devoted to their interests that President may be; whilst the thought irresistibly springs up in the mind—how degraded they must be in their own self-respect, when a whole people would flee to a single man at Washington to receive from him shelter and protection, when they have organized State governments of their own, which they might interpose, if they had only the courage to rouse up their slumbering energies.

The contingency, however, of either of the individuals just alluded to, filling the Presidential office, is so remote that it is scarcely worthy of the passing glance which we have given it. The pregnant, indisputable, momentous fact, which the South has now to deal with, is, that our enemies are about *to take possession of the Government*, that they *intend to rule us according to the caprices of their fanatical theories*, and according to the declared purposes of *abolishing slavery;* and that in working out these plans for our ruin and degradation, we must expect just that sort of leniency which is shown by the conqueror over a subjugated and craven people, who are the objects of his contempt and disgust, because they have proved themselves too cowardly to defend their honor, their families, and their property. Mr. Lincoln must be considered as the representative of these principles; and as soon and as long as they have control of the Government, it matters not to the South who fills the office of President. They have now so far the control, as to give to every Act of Congress a sectional character, and to defeat any measure of legislation friendly to the South. Upon the election of Mr. Lincoln they will take complete possession of the Government; and then they will carry out those schemes of hostility against our property and domestic peace, which they have long threatened us with, but which they have not had heretofore the power to accomplish.

Will the South remain a passive victim, and, like the timid sheep, allow itself to be bound whilst the butcher is preparing the knife for its destruction; or will she not rather throw off, at once, her degrading sloth and cowardice, and, summoning up her ample powers, throw off a government which is about to be taken possession of by her deadly enemies? If she decide this question according to the *wisdom of courage*, a long career of prosperity is before her, to be attained, perchance, through a sharp but brief conflict, which may call for much personal and pecuniary sacrifices; but if, on the contrary, she decide it according to the *folly of a timid sub-*

mission, her doom will be short as it will be dishonored ;—a few brief years of besotted indulgence, whilst their enemies are perfecting their plans:—then emancipation of their slaves; then poverty, political equal- ity with their former slaves, insurrection, war of extermination between the two races, and death, and expatriation, to fill up the picture.

How can Congress abolish Slavery in the States?

But it is asked, and that, too, sometimes, by intelligent men,—how can Congress abolish slavery, when the States alone in which it exists have control over it? The confidence with which this question is generally asked, would seem to imply that it can be answered only in the negative ; and that it can be abolished only with the consent of the owners of that property. Hence the indifference they manifest at the declared purposes of the Abolitionists to "extinguish it in every State of the Union." This dangerous mistake requires to be considered, and the modes by which that stupendous evil might be brought upon us, carefully reflected upon.

The two modes.

What, then, are the modes by which our enemies intend to abolish slavery in the South?

There are two modes by which this is to be done. The first is by *violence, insurrection* and *bloodshed.* The second is *"constitutionally,"* as they term it ; that is, through the operation of law, and a change of the Constitution, as soon as they get possession of the law-making power of the Government. The first is represented by the *Garrisonian wing* of the great Abolition party, of which Giddings, and Hickman, and Lovejoy, are the types, and such men as John Brown, and the miscreants who were lately hanged in Texas, are the agents. The second represents the *Black Republican* wing of the party, over which Seward is the master mind. Although differing in their modes of operation, the two wings of that great party are thoroughly identified in the mischievous *object* which they both aim at; and that is, the *entire abolition of slavery in the whole South !** The policy of the first, or Giddings and Garrisonian wing of the party, is to make slavery *unpopular* and *unprofitable,* by sending emissa- ries amongst our slaves, to excite them to insurrection and bloodshed, to burn down our towns and buildings of agriculture, to destroy our prop- erty, and lay waste our crops; and by the agitation and excitement which must accompany these measures, and by the poverty which it will spread over the whole South, to compel the slaveholder himself to eman- cipate his slaves. Mr. Giddings, of Ohio, many years ago, disclosed, in part, the programme of their operations, when, with the keen appetite for Southern blood which a fiend only could feel, he exclaimed : "I look for- ward to the day when there shall be a *servile insurrection* in the South ; when the black man, armed with British bayonets, and led on by British officers, shall assert his freedom, and wage a war of *extermination* against his master; when the *torch of the incendiary shall light up the towns and cities* of the South, and *blot out the last vestige of slavery.* And though I may not mock at their calamity, nor laugh when their fear cometh, yet I shall *hail it* as the dawn of a *political millennium.*" This man, let it be remembered, in passing, is the warm *personal* and *political friend* and supporter of Mr. Lincoln. Since he enunciated this scheme of assault upon our peaceful homes, his party have made additions to the instru-

---

* See Appendix, A.

ments of our destruction. To fire, and murder, and the devastation of property, they have added rape, and poison; and if they be permitted to accomplish their designs, we can expect from them in future nothing but the foulest indignities and the most atrocious cruelties.*

But, gentlemen of the Association, these evils can be arrested by vigilance and firmness: by vigilance in detecting every vile intruder upon our peace; and by firmness, in bringing the miscreant to condign and summary punishment, as soon as his guilt shall be established. In performing this duty to your families and to the State, I have the utmost confidence that the laws will be respected, and that nothing but even-handed justice will be dealt out to every one. Whilst we remain in the Union, our annoyances from these emissaries we may expect to be frequent, from the aid and sympathy which they will receive from a hostile government at Washington, and from the privileges they now have of travelling amongst us, as people under the same government. The time, however, I hope, is not distant, when they shall be deprived of these privileges and excuses, and they shall appear among us only as aliens and foreigners.

THE PEACEFUL AND CONSTITUTIONAL MODE OF MR. SEWARD.

The second mode, by which slavery is to be abolished, is that which Mr. Seward and his followers designate as " peaceful and constitutional." This is immeasurably a more dangerous scheme than that of open assault upon our institution, in the mode of insurrections; and nothing can save the South from the successful accomplishment of this scheme of our enemies, but her speedy separation from them; now that she has the power, and there are so many favorable circumstances to aid her in doing so. The danger with which this scheme is loaded, is so quiet and unobtrusive in its nature, that its advances will create little excitement or alarm in the South. It will possess itself stealthily of its victim. In the meantime, its cancerous roots will be spreading themselves over the whole system; causing the South daily to grow weaker, whilst the North is daily becoming stronger, by their exactions upon the South, and by the filling up of the Territories with an abolition population. And when, at the end of a few years, the South shall be waked up out of her drowsy lethargy, it will be to find that her power is gone, that the North has become her master, and can alter the Constitution to suit her own abolition purposes. In anticipation of a Black Republican President, Mr. Seward already begins to exult at the domination of the North, and over the impotency of the South. In a speech delivered by him on the 18th September, at St. Paul, Minn., in allusion to the warfare which has been waged upon African slavery by Black Republicanism, he boastfully exclaims: "The battle has been fought and the victory has been won.• Slavery to-day is, for the first time, not only *powerless*, but *without influence*, in the American Republic." This, it must be admitted, is a sober and humiliating fact, if the South were bound to remain in the Union, with a Black Republican and hostile government to rule over, degrade, and impoverish her. But with the right and the power to establish a government of her own (if God would only give her the wisdom and the courage so to determine), she might stand before the world, as proud a Republic as the sun now shines upon.

Regarding the South with the contempt which he and his followers have long learnt to indulge towards her, that under no circumstances of humiliation and injury can the South be "kicked out of the Union," Mr.

---

* See Appendix, B.

Seward knew well what he said, when he declared that slavery would be abolished, and that "constitutionally." To soothe the apprehensions of the South, to amuse them with delusive expectations, into a state of undisturbed confidence in the stability of their slave property, Mr. Seward seems to take particular pains, on all occasions, to make it known that the Black Republican party, which he controls, have no intention to disturb slavery in the States where it exists. An opposite declaration to this, he well knew would have alarmed the South, and perhaps driven some, or all of them, out of the Union, and then he would have lost the game. Not anticipating, apparently, that the Government at Washington could ever be turned over to the dominion of Abolitionism, and that slavery in the States could ever be overthrown, by any interference from that quarter, the people of the South generally regarded this annunciation of Mr. Seward, that it was to be abolished "constitutionally," with that sort of indifference with which men usually contemplate an impossibility. But the recent developments of the power of the Black Republican party, entertaining as it does, such deadly hostility to slavery, and hatred of slaveholders : with the certainty that it will soon control the whole power of the Government—is well calculated to disturb this equanimity, and stir up the inquiry, How can slavery in the States be "*constitutionally* abolished !"

The South, heretofore, has never had occasion, seriously to consider so momentous a question. Acting with the great Democratic party of the country (of which she has been, for several years past, the main support), and which has heretofore been constitutional and conservative in its aims, she has been able to protect her great institution of African slavery against the raging assaults of Abolitionism, so far, at least, as against any action coming from the General Government. The nomination of Fremont, four years ago, as a purely Northern and *sectional* candidate, was calculated to interrupt this serenity, as it indicated the advancing boldness of her enemies ; and the very small majority by which he was defeated, was a proof how rapidly their power had increased. Since then, squadron after squadron of Northern Democrats have turned traitors to the Constitution and their obligations to the South, and have deserted over to the enemy.

This gives to our enemies the victory—a victory which will be followed by a general stampede of the bulk of the Douglas Democrats, and of the Bell and Everett men, at the North (all at heart, Abolitionists), to take shelter within the enemy's camp, with a view to share with them in the spoils of the Government, and in the robbery of the South.

The South in a Hopeless Minority in the Government.

Let the South, then, face the reality, with such feelings as she may ; that she is now in a MINORITY, in the Federal Government ; a *minority* which will be *largely increased* with the result of the approaching Federal elections, which will leave the whole North banded with her enemies; a *minority* which will be *permanent*, and increasing year by year; a *minority* in a Government which is soon to be controlled by a party—one wing of which have sent, and are now sending among our people fire, and murder, and the sword, and rape, and poison, to desolate our land ; whilst the other wing is preparing and perfecting measures by the Government, to effect legally, and constitutionally, the "entire extinction of slavery in all the States." Let the South realize to herself, in all its dark and lowering aspects, the fact which Mr. Seward so triumphantly exults in,—"That slavery is now not only *powerless* but *without influence* in the American Republic."

Taking along with us in our minds this *fact* that the South is powerless to protect herself in the Federal Government, and that after the 4th March next she will be at the mercy of her enemies—the mercy of the Abolitionists—we are now prepared to consider intelligently the question : How Congress can abolish slavery in the States legally and constitutionally—at least according to the *forms* of law and the Constitution—which is all that the most lenient of our enemies will think it necessary to wait for.

In the first place it may be answered—this dire calamity cannot be inflicted upon the South *if she withdraw from the Union :*—whilst it can be, and inevitably will be, visited upon her, in all its horrors, if she continue connected with a Government which has both the will and the power to accomplish it.

An eloquent writer in Virginia has so forcibly presented the argument on this question, under the signature of " Python," in the March number of De Bow's excellent Review, that I make no apology for here availing myself of large extracts from it, and as also strengthening the views which I have previously expressed :

The manner in which " peaceful and Constitutional." Abolition, as it is called, will be accomplished.

"*Abolition proper* is founded on moral frenzy and religious fanaticism; and negating all law save that of a morbid imagination, all science save that of a diseased fancy, and all government save that of a prejudiced and infuriated mob, looks forward to the *social* and *political equality* of the negro with the white man, at whatever sacrifice of life and the industrial interests of the world, amidst rape, rapine, conflagration, robbery and murder. They have no statesmanship. They ignore the Constitution of the United States and all State Constitutions; and they declare the Union to be a '*compact with hell and an agreement with the devil.*' Woe unto the South! Woe unto the whole land, North as well as South, if the leaders of abolitionism, Giddings, Smith, Chase, Sumner, Wilson, Hale, Garrison, Phillips, Wilmot, Banks, Adams, Greeley, Bryant, and the '*three thousand Puritan preachers,*' should succeed in grasping the reins of Black Republicanism to guide that powerful organization in the line of their purposes. They would be governed alone by a blind rage in the subversion of the social, political and industrial systems of the South, *whether the South remained in the Union, or went out of the Union*, accompanied by the total loss of the cotton crop, thereby leading directly and inevitably to general starvation and anarchy through the destruction of manufactures. To the beastly horrors of the French Revolution in St. Domingo would be added the ghastly massacres of the French Revolution, and the squalid miseries of the great famine in Ireland.

Black Republicanism : what it is.

" *Black Republicanism*, embracing and *controlling Abolitionism*, on the other hand, *professes* to entertain due regard for law, government and constitutions. Mr. Corwin but repeats what Seward had previously said, even in his celebrated "irrepressible conflict" speech at Rochester, that whatever shall be done in reference to the subject of negro slavery, whether as the question affects the States or Territories, must be *constitutionally* done.* The present leaders of this party claim to respect

---

*The New York *Herald* thus substantiates this position in an article headed "The Issue before Congress and the country," viz :

" The issue before Congress and the country is the abolition of slavery in the slave States. *We know that Mr. Seward pleads the plea of a constitutional crusade;* but we know that constitutions and laws can be twisted into any shape by designing and reckless men. Helper and Brown are the true interpreters of the 'irrepressible conflict.' It means an aggressive conflict against slavery, a conflict of abolition forays from the free States, of servile revolts, of agrarian conspiracies, and the subjugation and suppression of slavery and the 'slave power' by terrorism, and by fire and sword."

9

all existing rights, political, real and personal. They all negate, orally and through their journals, the doctrines of the abolitionists proper. But they assert the constitutional supremacy of Congress over the territories, for the purpose of excluding negro-slave institutions, and thereby deny the right on the part of slaveholders to take to the territories, and hold therein, property in negro slaves. They moreover look forward with exultation and gratulation to the time, not very distant, when, through amendments to the Constitution constitutionally made, the slaveholding States themselves may be reached and controlled by Congress in the line of their real designs. As constructed and directed by Seward, their organization is political, and separate from religious fanaticism and moral frenzy; and so long as it remains political, is only potent for evil while the *South shall continue in the Union.* Nor are they destitute of policy and statesmanship. They have not only evolved a broad and profound policy, but have mentally eliminated a comprehensive and far-reaching statesmanship which contemplates, by the constant accession of 'free States' from 'free Territories,' and by a *continually accumulating and preponderating population, generating an overwhelming and all-controlling majority* of senatorial and popular representatives, the gradual *consolidation of the Government* through amendments to the Constitution thus to be wrought, and the *conversion of the confederacy into empire,* as necessary to the *suppression of rebellion and anarchy,* while preserving the *forms* of a representative republic, through clothing the President with dictatorial powers as aforetime was in Rome.

"Abolitionism, as we have said, governed by moral frenzy and religious fanaticism, has no stopping point; and Black Republicanism, in the hands of the abolition leaders, would pursue its objects at the South with all the fury of prejudice and rage of war after disunion. But Black Republicanism, as a political organization in control of abolitionism, has a stopping point, and ceases its power for *mischief in regard to the South, at least with disunion. On one point alone, is there absolute agreement between the two, and that is the ultimate property robbery of the South in respect to both real and personal estate;* and even here the means the one would resort to are different from those the other would pursue, as will presently appear.

INSECURITY OF PROPERTY AT THE NORTH AGAINST THE AGRARIANISM OF THOSE HAVING NO PROPERTY.

"A profound and thoughtful student of the annals of Tacitus, in their striking parallelism and application to our social and political condition, during that transition period when the old republic was passing into the empire of the Cæsars, without the alteration of a name or form that belonged to the ancient constitution—as may be readily ascertained from his extraordinary speeches—Mr. Seward set himself to the task of Marius and the great Julius, and under a liberal, generous, and magnanimous banner that equally appealed to every mass-element throughout the non-slaveholding States, attracted their regard, and *with a solitary exception hereafter to be honorably mentioned,* combined them all into that concentrated and powerful agrarian organization, called by themselves the 'Radical Democratic party,' but better known as 'Black Republican,' with himself as its apex. Long before this the *property* interests of the North had become alarmed at the daily increasing and overwhelming numbers and powers of the non-property holders enjoying the right of suffrage with property holders, and consequently, directing State legislation, so that all the burdens of government, civil and municipal, together with all the expenses of a general system of education, should be fastened upon property, *in itself unrepresented and without a voice in its own protection.* This had led to the earlier struggles in the national councils at Washington for the possession of the Territories by the North, and, finally, to that system of agrarian enactment, parceling out the public domains into 'free' farms for the multitude. These movements were intended by the representatives from the North to diminish danger at home, to secure their own doors, and to divert the hordes of agrarianism by supplying those necessities their will demanded. Regarding these facts, Seward, with the Black Republican party, now fully organized and returning a majority to Congress, resolved to hold, with an iron grasp, the Territories as against the South, and to *close in the slaveholding States* until the time should come when they would be demanded as a prey to feed the Northern vulture. *Hence he encouraged the Emigrant Aid Societies in their treason; hence he smiled approvingly upon Beecher, holding the Bible in one hand*

and Sharp's rifle in the other; hence his ceaseless diatribes concerning the aggressions of the South: hence his fervid denunciations of the Lecompton Constitution; and hence his studied defence of the Topeka outlaws in Kansas. He saw that, with the securement of Kansas as a non-slaveholding State, the doom of the South was sealed in the Union; that the slaveholding States, through the natural and constitutional flow of events afterwards, would necessarily become, first *provincialized* in a government they had contributed everything to form and sacrificed everything to maintain; and next, be driven, in some instances to relinquish their domestic institutions, and in others to submit to such changes as might be dictated by the North holding the Government, exercising its authority, and *wielding its power.* It was in view of all these designs of Black Republicanism and consequences to the South, that, two years ago, in January, 1858, during the pendency of the Kansas question, and while the South might yet have been rallied as a unit to prevent the threatened catastrophe, I addressed to their representatives in Congress the following appeal, to wit:

CONSEQUENCES OF THE LOSS OF KANSAS TO THE SOUTH.

"The surrender of Kansas to the operation of the *Majority Rule* in the Territories, under the cry of '*popular sovereignty*' without the Constitution, and her absorption by the non-slaveholding power of the country, will make the evil of the times no longer prospective, but *instant and imminent.* By the fact of this surrender the South will become subordinate and the North predominant in the Union. Never again in the Union, could the equilibrium of State-sovereign representation between the South and the North be either maintained in or restored to the Senate. Never again in the Union, could the equality of the South with the North be either maintained in, or restored to the House of Representatives. No further barrier could be constructed between either the aggressive Territorial, or the political rapacity of the North and the weakened and diminished South. The South, like the dead body of Hector bound to the car of Achilles, will soon be dragged by the triumphant North around a ruined possession, quickly to be followed by the erasive ploughshare of the subverting conqueror."

LOSS OF MISSOURI.

"The loss of Kansas to the South will involve the loss of Missouri, and the loss of Missouri will destroy the moral, as well as the political prestige of the South, and invade the integrity of their institutions. The moral prestige of States, like that of individuals, once destroyed, no earthly power can restore; and the integrity of State establishments, like the chastity of woman, once subjected to invasion, continues at the will of the despoiler. With abolitionized Iowa stretching along the northern boundary of Missouri, and abolitionized Kansas covering the western boundary, while through Kansas and Iowa there poured into her bosom, from the more inhospitable lake and northern Atlantic regions, a continuous stream of agrarian Radicals, alike determined to obtain control of her government and to assert the *rule of the majority* in the line of emancipation, slave property in Missouri will soon become too precarious in its tenure to be holden, and the necessity for its sale or removal will at once arise. It may be confidently asserted that, in a few years, Missouri, under these circumstances, will cease to be a slave-holding State. Already, in view of the anticipated result, Abolition journals have been started in Missouri, and some of her candidates for Congress have boldly unfurled the banner of emancipation.*

LOSS OF THE INDIAN TERRITORY.

"Now, the loss of Missouri to the South will involve the loss of the Creek and Cherokee domain, the Choctaw and Chickasaw domain, New Mexico and Arizonia, which otherwise could be saved to the slave-holding interests of the country and the harmonious equilibrium of the Union. It is known that the Creeks and Cherokees

---

* "One of these Abolition candidates has since been elected from the St. Louis district of Missouri. Such is the rapid advance of Abolitionism in that State."

number from thirty to forty thousand free inhabitants, holding at least ten thousand negro slaves. The facts as to the Choctaws and Chickasaws stand in a similar ratio. The white man's blood predominates in both nations, strongly coloring each with the mental forms and expressions of the white race. They have each a regular government, with distinct legislative, executive and judiciary departments; with a common-school system; with Christian churches established in many directions; and with the arts of Agriculture considerably developed. Each is gradually preparing to enter the Union as a slave-holding State. But with Abolitionized Kansas and Missouri (both being now subject to the North) along their northern limits, the flood gates will be thrown open through which the abolition tide will sweep with resistless energies, driving before it, or overwhelming in its deluge, alike the hybrid Indian and the negro slave, thus ultimately adding both domains to swell the colossal power of the North.* New Mexico and Arizona will now be thrown between the '*free soil*' States formed out of the territories of the Creeks, Cherokees, Choctaws and Chickasaws, on the east, the '*free soil*' States of California on the west, and the *free* States of Mexico on the South. Negro-slave property in neither could be held for a day, and they too will inevitably become incorporated in the monstrous proportions of the North.

Loss of Arkansas and Texas.

" In the next place, the loss of Kansas, of Missouri, of the Creek and Cherokee domain, of the Choctaw and Chickasaw domain, of New Mexico, and of Arizona, being a loss of six States rightfully belonging and legitimately attached to the slave-holding interest of the South, will involve the loss of Arkansas, another slaveholding State, and of Texas, warranted by the law of annexation, to be divided into five slaveholding States, thus making a positive loss to the South of twelve States, which in justice, as well as through a wise and politic statesmanship, should be saved to the slaveholding interest, looking to the future prosperity and welfare of the whole country, North as well as South, and subjecting to Abolitionism the entire western shore of the Mississippi river, reaching beyond the Rocky Mountains to the Pacific Ocean, and down to the Rio Grande, and convulsing Louisiana with servile war, saturating her soil with blood. With Kansas and Missouri abolitionized, and lying on the north and northwestern boundaries of Arkansas, and with Abolition States formed out of the Creek and Cherokee domain, and that of the Choctaws and Chickasaws, on her western limits, Arkansas will be circumstanced precisely as Missouri had been previously circumstanced, and negro slavery will be lost to Arkansas, in the same manner it had been lost to Missouri. No obstacle will now exist to the progress of the Abolition agrarian horde of the North, through Texas to the line of the Rio Grande. The great State, in point of geographical extent, is divided into three parts. Beginning on the shores of the Gulf of Mexico, the first division is a vast coast prairie, extending four hundred miles in length, from the Sabine to the Rio Grande, with an average width of forty miles. In addition to the two rivers mentioned, the Brazos, the Colorado, the Guadalupe, the Trinity, the San Antonio, and the Nueces, make their exit to the Gulf across this region, and within its bounds their waters may be said to be navigable. The soil is a black alluvial, the deposits of unnumbered ages, formed by the recession of the waters of the Gulf, and, for productiveness, equal to any in the world. Under a just expansion of the slaveholding, with the non-slaveholding interests of the country, here alone would be garnered as much cotton and sugar as are now obtained from the entire Union. The second division extends along the Red River and its streams, covering a space as large as that occupied by Virginia, and consists of a chocolate colored soil, well adapted to tobacco and the cereals, and favorably comparing with the richest grain-growing and tobacco lands of the earth. The

---

* " If the New York Tribune issued on November 7, the day of the last State election in New York, be referred to, it will be seen that that journal congratulates its own party upon the " forcible seizure of Kansas," and urges the same thing to be done with the Creek, Cherokee, Choctaw and Chickasaw country and New Mexico. The preachers of New England are now actively engaged in the Indian country striving to produce between the Indians bloody and exterminating strife ; by exciting their congregations against the slaveholders among them as " God abandoned, doomed to hell, and unfit to live." If blood could be once shed, extermination would be the result under the *lex talionis* that prevails, and thus the country would be left to the occupation of the ' Emigrant Aid Societies.'"

third division embraces the remainder of the State, in extent, four times the magnitude of Virginia, reposing on the upper waters of the rivers mentioned, and consisting, for the most part, of an elevated, rolling, and perfectly salubrious country. There is not to be found a region more productive in the natural grasses than this, and, consequently, it is not excelled for stock-raising purposes. Thus, in this magnificent State, spread out on the map, beneath a temperate sun, and in the midst of a genial clime, a glory and a blessing to the family of man, if left to legitimate and unforced settlement. But under the progress of precedent events and results, it must be seen that, with non-slaveholding States, formed out of the Indian Territory on her north, and out of New Mexico and Arizona on her west, while Mexico occupied her south, the *second* and *third* divisions will rapidly fill up with a *free soil* population, controlling the slaveholding population of the *first* division, and impelling and precipitating the negro slaves of that region into the ocean.*

Condition of Louisiana.

The situation of Louisiana will now be deplorable indeed. Surrounded on all sides save the east, by emancipated States, and with the negro slaves of Missouri, of Arkansas, of the Creek and Cherokee, Choctaw and Chickasaw domain, and of Texas, all massed down upon her as they were sold out, and placed beyond due restraint, because of the facilities afforded them to escape punishment by fleeing into the adjoining "free" States, and because of the magnitude of their number over that of her white citizens, Louisiana will inevitably fall a prey to internecine servile wars, so terrible that to live in their midst would be worse than to die, at the bare contemplation of which the mind shudders with horror.

"Nor are we permitted, yet, to rest our pen, in tracing the sequences that will follow to the South, from the loss of Kansas as a negro slaveholding State.

"While events are progressing to the fatal issues described, on the west of the Mississippi, others no less disastrous will be concomitantly evolved to the east, of that river. An extensive journey recently made through the Southern States, has enabled me to observe ocularly the fact, *that a non-slaveholding population, chiefly from the North, entertaining, for the most part, undisguised Abolition sentiments, predominates in the States of Delaware and Maryland; and that a numerous body of Northern born men inhabit the northern and western counties of Virginia, the eastern and northern counties of Kentucky, the western counties of North Carolina, the eastern and middle counties of Tennessee, and are to be found among the merchants of the cities of the Gulf coast, among the managers and employees of the Southern railroads, steamboats and hotels, and among the corps editorial, a majority of whom are Northern men holding, at present, suppressed sentiments, adverse to negro slavery, but ready, so soon as they attain to a popular majority, to speak out openly, in cooperating with the Abolitionists of the North.*

Loss of Maryland and Delaware.

"But it is my province here to look to facts as they are, rather than as I would they were; and looking to the facts before us, it is obvious that both Delaware and Maryland, in a few years, must yield to the abolition demon. The prestige of the South and the integrity of their institutions being invaded and destroyed in the manner indicated, the constant accumulation of Northern population, and concomitant accretion of abolition sentiment, in Delaware and Maryland, will compel them both to emancipation. Delaware, now, is only in name a slave State, and negro, slavery in Maryland is almost confined to two congressional districts, at the same time that she numbers an immense mass of 'free negros,' as a fruitful source of

---

* "Western Texas is already seriously threatened with being formed into a non-slaveholding State. The representatives of Texas entertain decidedapprehensions of the fact, and the Brownsville affair simply grows out of the fact that the Americans on the line of the Nueces, and between that river and the Rio Grande, *chiefly from the North*, have driven out the original Mexican inhabitants, now citizens of the United States, in order to get possession of their lands. I have had ocular demonstration, that a non-slaveholding population throughout that country are seeking to cut out a non-slaveholding State in that direction, south of slavery."

future insurrectionary trouble.* With the loss to the South of Kansas and Missouri on the *west*, and of Delaware and Maryland on the *east*, while the abolition States of Pennsylvania, Ohio, Indiana, and Illinois occupied the *north*, Virginia and Kentucky on the west, east and north. will become the recipients of an overwhelming non-slaveholding population, quickly swelling the numbers of non-slaveholders in those two States, into a ruling majority, and changing, as if by magic, their present deeply-felt, but only whispered, sentiments adverse to negro slavery, into loud thunders of indignation at the existence of the institution, and stern notes of defiance to the slaveholders. Virginia and Kentucky will thus be compelled to send out, or sell out, their slaves to the planting States, and surrender to the Moloch of abolition. To say nothing as to the effects of these things on the eight remaining slaveholding States, although it is evident they would be but as smoking flax in the fire, it must be seen that, *through the present loss of Kansas to the interests of the South, and the after-continuance of the Union, the South will lose sixteen States, legally, geographically and legitimately, their own, be shorn of their strength and glory and reduced to a cypher, with the whole burden of Resistance to Black Republican tyranny, wielding all the powers of an immense empire, resting on the planting States alone—a load so onerous that the combined powers of Europe, then in alliance, could hardly enable them to bear successfully.*

" Nor yet are these all the bitter fruits of the Union that the South will reap from the loss of Kansas, the more especially if the Black Republican party shall come to *grasp the government* with Seward as President. The North will be acquiring yearly new States from the territories, all of which are subject either to the law of popular sovereignty, or the simple majority rule, the local Mexican law, or to the Wilmot Proviso, as we have shown in the '*Territorial Status*', so that before all the sequences described are wrought out, the *non-slaveholding power in the government will become sufficiently great to amend the Constitution, under the terms of the instrument itself, investing Congress with full control over the subject of general emancipation.* Already with a majority of States in the Senate, and a preponderating voice in the House of Representatives, Minnesota, Oregon and Kansas are presented for admission as 'free States.' Others of similar character will rapidly follow from Washington, Dacotah, New Mexico, Arizona, Nebraska and Superior. *In a single lifetime, the constitutional requirements as to amendments will be met.*

" The mind accustomed to trace premises to their consistent conclusions, and to consider lines of causation with an analytic eye, cannot fail to see this to be no exaggeration. The Black Republican party, now in full possession of the North, declare themselves to be *crusaders in the cause of negro emancipation :* and I have heard leading Democrats even, men of character and renown at the North, assert, that '*they had carefully traced out the question with the map before them, and that in fifteen years there would be seventy non-slaveholding States to not more than ten slaveholding States in the Union.* And a distinguished gentleman of this party, a recent representative in Congress, from the city of Philadelphia, on Independence square, within the echoes of that hall where the declaration of our rights and the Constitution of the United States both had their birth, pandering to the general sentiments around him, asseverated, in allusion, we presume, to the ordinances of 1784-'7, the Missouri Compromise of 1819-'20, the Wilmot Proviso of 1848, the Compromises of 1850, and the Kansas-Nebraska Act of 1854, that '*every abolition triumph under the government had been achieved by the Democratic party.*' With the Black Republican party thus powerful, and the Democratic party thus demoralized, where may the South look for safety, friendship and support in the Union? Let them, for the future, *look only to themselves.* 'Who would be free, themselves must strike the blow.' Let them listen no more to the serpent voice of *Compromise*, neither trust to

---

* "There are ninety thousand free negros in Maryland, and an immense number of Northern men filled with abolition sentiments. The City of Baltimore, in the hands of 'Know Nothings', and represented in Congress by such men as Davis and Harris, who cooperate with the Black-Republicans, may be made the grand centre, at any moment, of the most bloody and terrible foray on the part of the Abolitionists, against the counties of the eastern and western shore that are slaveholding, for the purpose of expelling slavery from the State. If John Brown had made Baltimore the seat of his operations, and directed his movements against the country south of Baltimore, on both sides of the Bay, we are not prepared to say what the consequences and results would have been.

fillibustering raids for the acquisition of additional Southern territory. Let them firmly hold that which is now theirs, and boldly strike for that which should be theirs. Above all, let them never abandon Kansas as a negro-slaveholding State and as their *last* barrier, their *last* bulwark, and their *last* outpost against Northern encroachment and aggression. Then, perhaps they may save the *sixteen States* they will otherwise lose through the loss of Kansas and the *continuation of the Union* and thereby be enabled to advance with equal strides with the North. A course of firmness, of decision, of resisting determination and courageous action, *yielding nothing either to the spirit of peace or the demon of war*, is the only course by which the South may win or hold territorial rights, enforce the observance of the Constitution and the laws, erect a party on which they may repose with safety, and maintain their interests in the Union. Any other course is an abandonment of principle to false expediency, is an abnegation of self-respect, is the course of weakness and cowardice, of folly and poltroonery, and will court danger to pursue them, to overwhelm and to destroy them. Think not that Kansas can be lost to the cause of the South, and the South be saved from absorption by the North *in the Union.* If effect harmoniously follows cause, if the sequents of a mathematical problem flow consequentially from their antecedents to their ultimate conclusions, all the Southern States mentioned, one by one after the other, and all the deplorable results indicated, step by step in regular gradation, will march in funeral procession along the line of destiny, attendant upon the obsequies of the South, depicted by the leach of '*Compromise,*' and then struck dead by the galvanic shock of '*popular sovereignty and the majority rule.*'"

But we wrote and spoke in vain. In vain we endeavored to lay bare the issues between the North and the South, in their whole magnitude, in a speech delivered at Mobile during the fall of 1857, addressed to the "*Slaveholders of Alabama without distinction of party.*" The *leaders of the South continued absorbed in schemes of personal ambition,* and were circumscribed in their vision by the prospect of a mission to France, or a seat in the Cabinet, or the shadowy chance of a Presidential nomination in 1860. The comprehensive mind of Seward alone became impressed with the full aspect of the times. He not only saw that Kansas was the great turning point of the future— *and hence countenanced and defended the seizure of that territory by abolition outlaws through force of arms*—but also perceived that all the sequences detailed would *constitutionally* follow, and therefore, that the South, *if the abolitionists proper proceed wise,* would never be furnished legitimate ground or legal justification for disunion.

SLAVERY CAN BE ABOLISHED "CONSTITUTIONALLY" IN TEN YEARS.

Presuming the *Union to continue,* the thoughtful questioner of events cannot doubt that, *in ten years,* the North will hold, *sectionally,* the requisite *constitutional number of States,* senators and representatives, to enable them to propose and *adopt amendments to the Constitution* as they may please. The language of the Constitution upon the subject reads: "The Congress, whenever *two-thirds* of both Houses *may* deem it necessary, *shall propose* amendments to this Constitution, which *shall be valid* to all intents and purposes, as parts of this Constitution, when *ratified* by the legislatures of *three-fourths* of the several States, or by conventions in *three-fourths* thereof." Considering Kansas as already admitted, and Delaware as already attached to the Northern section, the Union stands composed of *twenty* non-slaveholding to *fourteen* slaveholding States, giving the first *forty* and the latter *twenty-eight* senators, and the first *one hundred and forty-nine* and the latter *eighty-nine* representatives. The gain of *two* free States by the North, and the loss of *two* slave States by the South, will increase the first to *twenty-four States with forty-eight senators,* and reduce the latter to *twelve States with twenty-four senators* which, at once, secures the requisite majority in the Senate to *propose* amendments. With a start of *sixty* majority in the House, and a white population in the proportion of *eighteen millions* to *six millions,* it cannot be long before the North shall obtain the requisite vote in the House. But *three-fourths* of the States are necessary to *ratify* proposed amendments. Will this be so difficult for the North to secure out of the immense territories altogether and exclusively at their disposal, through a large majority in both Houses or under the auspices of a Black Republican President? Would it not be an easy task for Seward, under these circumstances, to cut up the territories into from twenty to fifty

States, and to bring them into the Union with fractional populations, even, so as to procure the constitutional number required? The question presents a fact too plain for argument, and the treasons of Kansas and Harper's Ferry do not permit the mind to halt in its conviction because of the *immoral* nature of the proceeding. But without this, recurring to our argumentative appeal above quoted, as submitted to the senators and representatives from the South during the Kansas issue, it must be seen that the ceaseless *accumulation of Northern population*, and the *legitimate accessions of Northern States from the territories*, combined with the *rapid subversion of Southern States in the Union*, will surely accomplish, in this respect, within the time designated, all the aspiring anticipations of Seward, and chain the South to the triumphant car of his ambition.*

It is only necessary to give to these extracts the careful examination which the profound importance of the question is entitled to, for any reflecting mind to be convinced that the Abolitionized States will have the power, within a very few years, to *alter the Constitution in any way they please;* and so fulfil the intentions of Mr. Seward and his Black Republican colleagues, of "abolishing slavery in all the States in a constitutional manner." Whether this shall be allowed to be done *at all*, will depend upon the South: or whether it shall be done within the time indicated by this Virginia writer, (ten years,) or whether it be delayed some five or ten years longer, does not affect the question of their power, sooner or later, to do it. That they will do it within the shortest practicable time, we may certainly expect, when we consider that it has been for years the object of their earnest labor and ardent desires; and when it is considered that we are regarded by them as powerless in their hands and as too cowardly to resist.

SLAVERY MAY BE ABOLISHED BY "LAW," IN THE FORTS, DOCKYARDS, &c.

But, if we consent to submit to a hostile government to make laws for us, there is a measure which does not require an *alteration of the Constitution*, to be put in force against us, but within any five days after Mr. Lincoln's inauguration into office, may be passed through its three readings and its committees, and stand out upon the statute book a duly enacted "law," bristling with the most formidable armory of mischief—encouraging discontent and insubordination among the slaves, and entailing incalculable losses upon their owners. I allude to a law "to abolish slavery in the forts, arsenals, dockyards, and other places in the South, where Congress has exclusive jurisdiction."

This has long been a cherished scheme of the Abolitionists for annoyance and injury to the South, but they have hitherto never had the power to carry it into effect. What does it mean? Their aim is not, surely, limited to the emancipation of the few slaves who may be found in those places, in the capacity of body-servants to the officers and their families, amounting in numbers, at most, only to a few dozen negros. Their scheme is much deeper, more mischievous, and fraught with infinite danger to the South. It is, by abolishing slavery in those places, to impart to them the *character of free soil territory*—to make our forts, arsenals and dockyards, the asylums and harbors, of refuge to every disaffected slave who may retreat to them, and who, being within the jurisdiction of a *free soil territory*, may claim his freedom in the same manner as is now done in free soil Massachusetts or Vermont. Cast the eye over the map, from Baltimore to Galveston, in Texas, and note the forts, navy yards and

---

* See Appendix, C.

arsenals which dot the whole South, and then contemplate the consequences of making all these the asylums for deluded or disaffected slaves, and where papers of emancipation were to be had only for the trouble of going there to receive them. What subordination could be preserved among the slaves within the cities of Norfolk, Wilmington, Charleston, Savannah, Pensacola, Mobile, New Orleans, or upon the plantations for a hundred miles around, of which each of these was a focus—if the slave, for any fancied grievance, could leave his master and find security, and release from his service, within the walls of a fort. Any sudden petulance occasioned by some mild, but well-deserved rebuke or punishment, would be resented upon the master; and a walk of twenty minutes to some contiguous dockyard, or a voyage of a few miles in a paddling canoe, to some fort within sight, would take him to *free soil*, where the master would be powerless in retaking him.

SLAVE COULD NOT BE RECOVERED.

But some innocent might say, he ought to be given up. By whom? Is it expected that it will be done by Abolition officers, commanding Abolition soldiers, all selected by an Abolition President and Commander-in-Chief, for the express purpose of enforcing the policy of the law, and *not* giving him up.

Another innocent may urge that he must forcibly be arrested and returned to his master. By what process? The Fugitive Slave law (that delusion and snare,) will have been repealed; for who believes that it will be allowed to remain upon the Statute book, six months, after the Black Republicans shall have got possession of the Government. The only remaining civil process is that through the State Courts of the South. But the very purpose of the law was to *emancipate the slave*, and deprive the master of his use; and there stands the fort which shelters him, manned with Abolitionists to carry out this purpose, and bristling with cannon frowning upon the Sheriff and his posse. The State now in her capacity of a sovereign, must interpose; or make the humiliating confession before the world that she is incompetent to protect her own citizens from insult and injustice. How immeasurably better for her, had she taken this step from the outset, by throwing off the authority of that hostile Government, before it had made these dangerous lodgments within her boundaries, or before she had conferred upon it the right, by having submitted to its rule, to pass laws so ruinous to our safety and honor!

NO STATE OF THE SOUTH CAN PERMIT THIS.

But no State of the South could, consistently with her own dignity, and with the duty she owes of protection to her citizens, permit such a law to take effect within her bounds. To allow these *nests* of Abolitionism to be established within her population, from which, as radii from so many centres, "under-ground railroads" (so called) might diverge to every city, town, and plantation within a hundred miles or more around, bearing our deluded slaves to these dockyards and forts; then to be made free, and thence to be transferred to the free soil North, where, after the fugitive slave law is abolished, concealment and "under-ground railroads" would then no longer be necessary, but the absconding slave would walk abroad in open day—to allow such a law (to be followed by such consequences,) to *operate* within the boundaries of any Southern State, would, I say, be equivalent to a declaration on her part, that she was unable or unwilling to protect the slave property of her citizens, and that they were at the mercy of every daring spoliator and fanatic. Abolition of slavery would, in such cases, already have begun by this *law* of an Abolition Congress; and it would not be necessary to wait the brief respite of *ten years* to do it "constitutionally." That the Abolitionists do not limit their views (as some might try to persuade themselves,) to the paltry effects of emancipating the few slaves before alluded to, which may now be found in these forts and dockyards—on which supposition "the play would not be worth the candle"—but that they intend to extract from that law the ruinous consequences, such as I have described, is sufficiently proved by the earnest zeal with which they have always pressed for the passage of such a law. Let the South, then, with equal earnestness, be prepared to meet this formidable danger.

How can the abolition of Slavery in the Forts, Dockyards, &c., be avoided?

How can this be most wisely done—in the Union, or out of the Union? If in the Union, it is not too much to say, that no matter, through what several processes the controversy may pass, (and it will be venturing little to predict that our Abolition enemies will be triumphant in all), it must, in the last resort, terminate in a collision *of force* between the two governments;—that is, if the Southern State really intends to protect her citizens in the possession of their slaves. Thus will come upon us the "collision" which is so much dreaded by the timorous, that they seem willing to postpone, or avoid it altogether, by every unmanly delay or suicidal compromise;—a "collision" which, if we remain in the Union, may be precipitated upon us within any *brief period* after Mr. Lincoln's inauguration into office, allowing only time enough for such a law to be prepared and enacted; and lastly a "collision" which we shall have to meet in the worst form, in which we can join battle with our enemies—that, in which a State, after having *submitted* to the detestable rule of her enemies, is afterwards found in armed resistance to that government;—under which circumstances, the words "treason," and "rebel," and "rebellion," have an intelligible and very ominous signification.

But if we consider the consequences of such a law, in its effects upon us, as sovereign and independent States, *having no connexion* with the abolitionized government which has passed it, all these dangers instantly vanish. Having withdrawn from their government, they have no right any longer to make laws for us. Having withdrawn the authority which we imparted to them over certain territory, for *friendly* and *federal* purposes, and having, in the exercise of our undoubted right as a sovereign, spread our jurisdiction over every inch of ground within our territorial limits, they have no longer any territory *within our boundaries* over which they can execute their laws. We stand to them, then, in all political relations, as France does to England—independent and sovereign; in which coercion and armed collision may mean war, but in which the words "treason" and "rebellion" cease to have any application or meaning.

If, then, the South would escape the dire effects of the abolition of slavery, whether it is to be inflicted upon us by the comparatively tardier course of a *change of the Constitution*, or may be begun within a very few months by *law*, abolishing it in the forts, dockyards, &c.,—the best attitude in which she can meet the danger is that of a separate and independent gov-

D2

ernment and as having control of the subject, and ready to deal with it a friendly and not hostile spirit.

And to those who are so timorous lest the secession of one or more States of the South might provoke collision, it would be well to suggest the inquiry whether such collision would not arise more certainly, and just as soon, *within the Union*, from the necessity of defending our citizens against a law so ruinous as the one for abolishing slavery in our forts, magazines and dockyards. Considered, then, in the light of a mere timid policy, nothing can be gained, whilst numberless advantages will be lost by *postponing* the time of vigorous resistance; especially as the question *must be decided* within a very few years, whether we shall secede and fight for our rights, or allow *slavery to be abolished* by an alteration of the Constitution.

The Abolition of Slavery!! Consider the words!

The abolition of slavery in all the South, with all its unspeakable calamities, and its incalculable losses! What a price the cowardly submissionist is willing to pay for a few years of ignoble sloth, vouchsafed to him by his enemies! And how stupendous is his *folly*, which, after having paid such a price, finds that he has obtained, not a release, but only a *brief respite;* and that he must, at last, encounter "secession," "collision," and "coercion," under much worse circumstances, or give up his slaves to emancipation, his family to degradation, his property to ruin and himself to poverty.

The abolition of slavery! Have any of you, gentlemen, *deliberately* reflected upon the import of the thing, and run it out, through all its sad dening consequences? I ask the question because I have seen so many people speak of it as a thing which is to come; but with a species of torpid insensibility, as if it was to come *without consequences.* Let us, then, bestow a few thoughts upon what the "Abolition of Slavery" means.

Loss of all agricultural Slave labor.

In the first place, it means the annihilation and end of all negro labor (agricultural especially) over the whole South. I mean that regular, steady, *continuous* labor from the beginning to the end of the year, and year after year, without which agriculture in the South cannot be carried on successfully, if it can be carried on at all. I am now, gentlemen, addressing an association of planters, who know that this proposition is true without dispute. Plantation work is, you know, composed of a succession of employments, each depending upon the other, like the several links of a chain;—the neglect of any one of which employments (like the breaking of one link in the chain), renders useless all the work which has previously been performed, and entails a loss of the whole crop. As planters, no one knows better than you, how useless it would be to plough, to dig, and to *prepare* your land, if you had not labor afterwards to *plant* it—how useless, again, to prepare the land, and plant it, without the labor necessary afterwards to *hoe* and *cultivate it;* and how useless it would be to do all these several works, if there were no labor at command to *gather the crop.* It is the absurd notion of the pragmatical, conceited Abolitionist, who thinks he knows more of other people's business than they know themselves,—to fancy that agriculture, at the South, can be carried on as well with *hired* (and therefore irregular) labor, as with *compulsory* labor. It is from acting upon this senseless theory, that all negro labor has been destroyed in the British West Indies, in Peru, and everywhere else, where the theory has been tried, and that those colonies are reduced to poverty and worthlessness. "It is a fact," says the London *Times*, in reviewing the late work of Mr. Trollope, on the British West Indies,—" it is a fact that half the sugar estates and more than half the coffee plantations have gone back into a state of *bush*, and a great portion of those who are now growing canes in Jamaica are persons who have lately bought the estates for the value of the copper in the sugar boilers, and of the metal in the rum stills." Such is the enormous depreciation of real estate in the West Indies, by the emancipation of the slaves, and by substituting in the place of *compulsory* slave labor, the irregular, *hired* labor of the *freed* negro, which, from its uncertainty, is no labor at all suitable to the planter. What would your condition be with such laborers, if, in mid-valley of your summer work, when the crop, and the grass too, were in vigorous growth, your *hired*, *freed*-negro-gang (your "equals" and "fellow-citizens," by the "grace" of law and the Abolitionists) should throw their hoes upon their shoulders, and say to you that they would work no longer, except you trebled or quadrupled their wages? Why, the only wise thing which you could do, would be, at once, to give up the crop, which perhaps would not pay the expenses. And so it would be at any other stage of its cultivation.

It is undoubtedly true, then, that the abolition of slavery at the South means the annihilation of all negro labor; and with the loss of that labor, the end of all crops; and with loss of crops, the end of all income to the planters.

Loss of 9,000,000,000 of property to the Whites.

It means, next, a loss to the planters of the South of, at least, ($4,000,-000,000,) four thousand millions of dollars, by having this labor taken from them: and a loss, in addition, of ($5,000,000,000) five thousand millions of dollars more, in lands, mills, machinery, and other great interests, which will be rendered valueless by the want of slave labor to cultivate the lands, and the loss of the crops which give to those interests life and prosperity.

The reign of Negro sloth and idleness.

It means, again, the turning loose upon society, without the salutary restraints to which they are now accustomed, more than (4,000,000) four millions of a very poor and ignorant population, (as the peasantry of most countries are,) to ramble in idleness over the country until their wants should drive most of them, first to petty thefts, and afterwards to the bolder crimes of robbery and murder; or until their excesses, their imprudence, their filth, and starvation, shall bring pestilence amongst them and sweep them off by thousands. Improvident to the last degree, as they are, and accustomed to have all their wants carefully attended to, day by day, would find them without provision; which, night by night, they must supply by the plunder of stock, and of every other thing which they could carry off; until the country would be laid waste and impoverished by their interminable aggressions.

The equality of the negro with the white race.

But the abolition of slavery means, further, that the negro is not only to be made free, but *equal* also to his former master, in political and civil rights; and, as far as it can be done, in social privileges. The planter and his family are not only to be reduced to poverty and want, by the robbery of his property, but to complete the refinement of the indignity, they are to be degraded to the level of an inferior race, be jostled by them in their paths, and intruded upon, and insulted over by rude and vulgar upstarts. Who can describe the loathsomeness of such an intercourse;—the *constrained intercourse* between refinement reduced to poverty, and swaggering vulgarity suddenly elevated to a position which it is not prepared for? It has heretofore resulted in a war between the races, and the extermination of one or the other; or it has become so intolerable, that expatriation has been preferred as an evil more easily to be borne.

The abolition of Slavery; with "compensation" for the Slaves

I have considered that the abolition of slavery, when it shall be inflicted upon the South, by a change of the Constitution—whether it is to take place in ten, or twelve, or fifteen years—will be done *absolutely*, without anything to mitigate it, and without *any compensation* to the owners of the slaves. There is nothing to encourage the expectation that it will be done in any other way. "Python," however, in the article in *De Bow's Review*, from which we have already made extracts, thinks that they will be "bought" (or rather taken) from the planters, by the Government, at a hundred dollars per head; retained by the Government for ten years, as "apprentices," and hired out, to "pay back their purchase money." Under this more mitigated form of abolition (in which, however, I think he will find himself mistaken), he nevertheless portrays, with his graphic pen, the gloomy consequences, in language following:

"In a pecuniary point of view, the Southern planters are, for the most part, in a similar condition to the planters in the British West India Colonies, prior to the British act of emancipation. That is to say, almost every estate at the South, now valued at two hundred thousand dollars, equally divided between land and machinery on the one side, and negro slaves and live stock on the other, is incumbered with a debt, by way of mortgage or otherwise, of at least twenty thousand dollars. The average price of *one hundred dollars per head* allowed by the Government for the slaves, being only *one-tenth* part of their real value, will reduce the one hundred thousand dollars of personal estate to ten thousand dollars; and as this sum would not be payable in cash, but only in Government bonds, bearing legal interest, and could not be made available as cash, except at a great sacrifice, the real sum derived to the planter, for practical purposes, would be simply the annual interest on ten thousand dollars, or an income tax of six hundred dollars per year. The indebtedness or incumbrances of the planter will now fall entirely on his real estate and machinery;—and how will they be effected? The planter being alike unaccustomed to the 'apprentice system,' and unwilling to hire as apprentices, those whom he had owned as slaves, will be loth to engage from the agents of the Government the requisite force for the cultivation of his lands and the employment of his machinery. Least of all could he, grounded as he must necessarily be in the mild morals of the patriarchal system of slavery and labor subsisting at the South, reduce himself to countenance and practice a harsh code and procedure like that eliminated by Great Britain and France from the *driving system* of labor, associated with that worse than Egyptian bondage, the 'Apprentice system.' His lands and machinery will thus be, unavoidably and immediately, with the fact of emancipation, reduced in a similar ratio to his personal estate, and sold under the sheriff's hammer, as was the case in the British Colonies. His estate of two hundred thousand dollars, enabling him to live in affluence and to educate his children in mental and physical refinement, will thus be curtailed to twenty thousand dollars, one half of which will be unavailable, leaving his indebtedness to swallow up his last dollar. Or if, perchance, he should be free from indebtedness, he will never consent to the new order of things, but will rather sell his lands and machinery for anything to be obtained for them, and fly from the graves of his ancestors to some unknown spot in the wilderness, where his susceptibilities cannot be wounded. But whether his lands and machinery be sold out by the sheriff, or he shall voluntarily sell them, the end to him will still be the same. From wealth he will be reduced to want, and his children to beggary. His family will become dispersed; the places that once knew him will know him no longer; and his memories, even, will perish, save as future ages may darkly divine them, from the page of history."

To the above, "Python" adds the following note:

"The author has now in his possession a vial of laudanum, which he took from the oldest son of a former Governor of the Island of Barbadoes, in order to prevent him from committing suicide, by reason of the poverty to which he had been reduced by the British act of emancipation. His father was Governor of the Island of Barbadoes at the time the act of emancipation went into effect. At that time he was the wealthiest planter in the Island. His estate was somewhat encumbered, but the encumbrance was not felt until emancipation. Then suddenly it swallowed up the whole estate, except a mere remnant. He died broken-hearted, and his son came to Philadelphia in search of employment. His little means failed him before he succeeded, and with his last dime he determined to seek consolation in death. Being at the same boarding house with him, I prevented the catastrophe, and got him sent back to Barbadoes through the aid of several kind-hearted merchants, who traded with the Island, and knew his father well. This case directly illustrates the condition to which the planters of the South and their children will be reduced by Black Republicanism, after its designs shall have been fulfilled."

This, then, gentlemen, is the sad import of the "abolition of slavery" in the South—the end of all negro labor; a jubilee of idleness, and a reign of sloth; until famine shall drive them to robbery, or scourge them with pestilence: nine thousand millions of property destroyed, belonging to the white race, in return for negro equality conferred upon the black race: a war of races; the subjection of one or the other; certain poverty to the whites; degradation, want, expatriation.

THE EFFECTS OF ABOLITION IN LOSS OF INCOMES—TO THE PLANTER, MERCHANT, FACTOR, &c.

Viewed in its merely pecuniary aspects, we have seen that it makes an end of crops and the incomes of planters. And as this is the great treasure-house from which all other interests draw their supplies, it may be inquired, without crops what becomes of the factors, the railroads, the shipping, and all the interests dependent upon these. Without incomes to the planters, what becomes of the merchant, the machinist, the mechanic? The planter would be too poor to buy the goods of the one, or to need or employ the services of the other; but all would sink into one common ruin. In speaking of these we have allusion only to those who, whether native born or adopted citizens, have cast in their lot with the South; who are bound permanently to the soil by their property or the ties of family, and who have made it the permanent home of their choice.

We allude not to those Northern merchants from Abolitionized States who leave their Northern *homes* for the winter merely to *do business at the South*, intending, with the return of the swallows, to go back to their *Northern homes*, taking with them all they have gleaned at the South, and spend these copious profits among their *Abolition friends* and *neighbors*. We allude not to those adventurers who annually come on to the South from those regions of fanaticism, merely rent a room or store for a few months, in one of our towns, and then, from the sign of a "Little Shoe," or "Big Boot," or under the firm of "Sumner Brother," or, "Seward, Giddings & Lincoln," spread out their goods upon the counter to extract money from our people, whilst they are spreading Abolitionism in the back room by *lectures* and *pictures*.

We allude to none of such people among our merchants as being likely to be injured *with us* by the Abolition of slavery. *They* have no sympathies in common with us—no ties which bind them to the South except the most fragile threads of *making money* out of us. They are indifferent to the honor, the safety, the permanent welfare of the South. All that they concern themselves about is to prevent anything from being done which may *interrupt their business* of making money out of us. Accordingly, upon every effort of the South to breast the dangers which beset us, and break the fetters with which we are bound, we find them at all elections banded with the submissionists, multiplying the alarms of the timid, and pulling the South down to non-resistance and dishonor. Abolition of slavery (if they do not at heart desire it) affects them very slightly. Whilst the merchant, the mechanic, the machinist whose *home* is the *South*, must sink into the common ruin which Abolition of slavery will bring upon the South, *this* Northern merchant has nothing to do but to gather up his profits, pack up his boxes, betake himself to some steamer, and in five days, or less, he is at *home* among his *Abolition friends*, but our bitter enemies!

The Effects upon the Non-Slaveholder.

We forbear to notice the effect of the abolition of slavery upon the Banks, Insurance Companies, Railroads, and all other corporations, depending upon a rich and flourishing country for their own prosperity. But in noticing its effects upon the different classes and interests in the South, we should not omit to notice its effects upon the *non-slaveholding* portion of our citizens.

Accompanied as that measure is to be, by reducing the two races to an *equality*—or, in other words, in elevating the negro slave to an equality with the white man—it will be to the non-slaveholder, equally with the largest slaveholder, the obliteration of *caste* and the deprivation of important privileges. The color of the white man is now, in the South, a title of nobility in his relations as to the negro; and although Cuffy or Sambo may be immensely his superior in wealth, may have his thousands deposited in bank, as some of them have, and may be the owner of many slaves, as some of them are, yet the poorest non-slaveholder, being a white man, is his superior in the eye of the law; may serve and command in the militia; may sit upon juries, to decide upon the rights of the wealthiest in the land; may give his testimony in Court, and may cast his vote, equally with the largest slaveholder, in the choice of his rulers. In no country in the world does the poor white man, whether slaveholder or non-slaveholder, occupy so enviable a position as in the slaveholding States of the South. His color here admits him to social and civil privileges, which the white man enjoys nowhere else. In countries where negro slavery does not exist, (as in the Northern States of this Union and in Europe,) the most menial and degrading employments in society are filled by the white poor, who are hourly seen drudging in them. *Poverty*, then, in those countries, becomes the badge of inferiority, and wealth of distinction. Hence the arrogant airs which wealth there puts on, in its intercourse with the poor man. But in the Southern slaveholding States, where these menial and degrading offices are turned over to be performed exclusively by the negro slave, the status and *color of the black race* becomes the badge of inferiority, and the poorest non-slaveholder may rejoice with the richest of his brethren of the white race, in the distinction of his color. The poorest non-slaveholder, too, except as I have before said, he be debased by his vices or his crimes, thinks and feels and acts as if he was, and always intended to be, superior to the negro. He may be poor, it is true; but there is no point upon which he is so justly proud and sensitive as his privilege of caste; and there is nothing which he would resent with more fierce indignation than the attempt of the Abolitionist to emancipate the slaves and elevate the negros to an equality with himself and his family. The abolitionists have sent their emissaries among that class of our citizens, trying to debauch their minds by persuading them that they have no interest in preventing the abolition of slavery. But they cannot deceive any, except the most ignorant and worthless. The intelligent among them are too well aware of the degrading consequences of abolition upon themselves and their families (such as I have described them), to be entrapped by their arts. They know that at the North and in Europe, where no slavery exists, where poverty is the mark of inferiority; where the negros have been put on an equality with the whites, and "money makes the man," although that man may be a negro—they know, I say, that there the white man is seen *waiting* upon the negro;—there he is seen *obeying* the negro as his ostler, his coachman, his servant and his bootblack. Knowing, then, these things, and that the abolition of slavery, and the reign of negro equality here, may degrade the white man in the same way as it has done in those countries, there is no non-slaveholder in the South, with the spirit of the white race in his bosom, who would not spurn with contempt this scheme of Yankee cunning and malice.

THE EFFECT OF ABOLITION UPON THE SLAVES THEMSELVES.

The abolition of slavery over the South well deserves to be considered, also, in its effects upon the slaves themselves. And here it may be confidently predicted (what future history will certainly verify) that, should it ever take place, it will bring to them none of the advantages which our enemies so insanely anticipate. It has not benefitted them yet in any country in which it has been tried; except their relapsing into their native barbarism, sloth and besotted superstition and ignorance, may be considered as an advantage. It has been a failure in Peru, in St. Domingo, in the British Colonies in the West Indies—than which no places on the globe could have been selected more favorably for the experiment;—a tropical climate, requiring little expense for clothing, and affording, all the year round, a season for growing food; an immensely fertile soil, abounding in fruits of spontaneous growth, and yielding abundance of food with little labor; a powerful government giving them protection, and preventing any interference from without in their progress in civilization and the useful arts. Having entire control of the country, by a ratio in numbers of twenty-five, to one, over the whites, and, therefore, with nothing within, to arrest their improvement, if there were in the nature of their race any self-acting principle for improvement;—and yet what has been the result? In things *praiseworthy*, nothing; absolutely nothing!

A CRIME AGAINST THE SLAVE AS WELL AS THE MASTER.

What, then, can we expect from the emancipation of the slaves at the South, with not one of these advantages; and with all the natural imbecility of the race still inherent in them? With a climate comparatively harsh and ungenial, and with a soil yielding no food spontaneously, and from which food and the means of clothing are to be extracted only by toil; with no intelligence to stimulate their industry and to direct their labor, the consequences flowing from their idleness and improvidence will be such as have been described,—starvation and disease. With the restraints of the mild, but ever-acting *plantation police* withdrawn from them; slothful, thriftless and without forethought, a very few years would find them a sottish, thieving, ragged *lazzaroni*—a nuisance to the country, and the pests of every neighborhood. The swaggering insolence of their new-born equality would soon make them intolerable, to even the poorest white man; and when to this is added the festering irritation which shall have been kindled by their numerous vices and their crimes, there will be a general uprising among the whites of all classes to drive them out of the country. Thus will commence that war between the races, which every reflecting mind perceives to be inevitable, where an inferior and degraded race has been *forced up*, by foreign interference, to an equality with their former master race. In such a war, with the whites well armed, and acquainted with their use, and double in number to the blacks, who doubts the result? Horrible tragedies may be enacted in a few neighborhoods; but it must soon terminate in the indiscriminate slaughter of the negros, by tens of thousands and hundreds of thousands, until they shall be either exterminated, or driven out of the country. The late insurrection in British India comes in here, as an illustration, and proof of two things: 1st, that an inferior and superior race cannot live together in the same country on terms of *equality;* and 2d, that in the struggle for ascendancy, although the inferior race was, perhaps, fifty times more numerous, they were in due time completely subdued by the superior intelligence and courage of the white man. And such will be the doom of the negros of the South, in any war with the whites. How stupendous, then, is the folly and crime of the Abolitionist, who, under pretence of benefitting the slave, would plunge him down into so misc able a doom!

See the folly and *crime* of such intermeddlings. He finds a slave population, who, he works himself up to believe, must be very miserable; but who, in fact, are as comfortable and free of care as any laborers in the world. He carries fire, and poison, and pikes, and fire-arms, stealthily among them; and tries to persuade them to terminate their miseries by rising up and murdering their masters. But they cannot be persuaded that they are miserable. A few sullen or credulous ones may be reluctantly persuaded to receive the arms or the poison; and as long as the crime which they are incited to commit may be at a distance, they may, with a troubled conscience, consent to keep them. But the slaves are not the brutes and savages which the Abolitionists suppose them to be. God has placed consciences in their bosoms; they have the common feelings of humanity in their hearts; many of them are governed by the holy precepts of Christianity, and understand the duties of "obedience" which God has enjoined that the slave show to their masters. Many of them, again, have been brought up in the families of their masters; have been the companions of their childhood and youth, and have acquired a sincere friendship and attachment for them; whilst there is scarcely one of them who cannot recall to mind many faults forgiven, and numerous favors conferred. No one, then, in the South, at least, is surprised that when the day draws near, when the dark and bloody deed is to be *committed* that some faithful friend among the slaves repudiates the plot, and discloses the treason; and that even those who have, at the beginning consented to receive the arms, now, with a stricken conscience, shudder to make use of them. It is only the Abolitionist who is surprised at such a termination of his diabolical plans. He thought that in dealing with slaves, he was dealing with brutes; he now finds that they are men, having in their hearts the feelings of humanity.

But the deed has been done, and now the melancholy consequences are at hand! The plot has been concocted, and the Abolitionist has involved in it many a poor slave who has thoughtlessly consented to join in it, and who has not afterwards withdrawn himself from it. The Abolitionist is arrested and hung; and with him, unhappily, the poor, deluded, ignorant slaves also, whom he has entrapped in his plot. Whilst their doom is but just, the slaves of the South, under the artful temptation of the Abolitionists, are now, real objects of commiseration to the white race of the South. If let alone they would live with us all the days of their life in harmony, and with the kindliest good offices. I have not a distrust of them if left to themselves. The Abolitionist is the enemy of the master; but he is the more deadly enemy to the poor slave who listens to his artful persuasions. The late insurrections is Texas prove this. Whilst in that State, perhaps fifteen Abolitionists have been hung for planning these insurrections, perhaps eighty, if not more, negros, who foolishly agreed to join them, have already also been hung; whilst not a slaveholder in Texas has had a hair on his head injured. The deaths and the misery have then fallen chiefly upon the deluded, unfortunate slaves who have joined the Abolitionists; and this is the melancholy fact in every other place where the Abolitionists have attempted insurrection,—the negros only have been the victims.

The fact, then, is indisputable, that the abolitionist, whether he intends it or not, is the greatest enemy of our slaves, and they cannot too soon be warned of their danger, so as to avoid his temptations, and escape being entrapped by him.

INSURRECTION NOT SO MUCH TO BE DREADED AS THE ACTION OF A HOSTILE GOVERNMENT HAVING THE POWER OF MAKING LAWS FOR THE SOUTH.

Let us, then, gentlemen of the Association, endeavor to protect our slaves, as well as ourselves, against those diabolical schemes of the abolitionist. Ordinary vigilance, followed by prompt punishment when the guilt is plain, will effect this. With this vigilance I have no serious apprehensions for the safety of our institutions, from *insurrection*. My apprehensions spring from the operation of laws, and the alteration of the constitution, which will steal upon us so gradually as to shear us of our locks, before the Philistines come upon us. The policy of Mr. Seward is that which is most to be dreaded,—that cautious policy which will do nothing to startle the South (ever too prone to temporizing) and which may *drive her from the Union;* than which, nothing would carry more disappointment and dismay to Mr. Seward and the Black Republicans; for then, the South would be safe, and the abolitionized North have lost their victim.

The Presidential Election over, a Great Southern Party must be formed, to save the South.

Let us congratulate ourselves, gentlemen, that the Presidential election will soon be over, and the miserable scramble about men be at an end. What is Mr. Bell, or Mr. Breckinridge, or Mr. Douglas, with all the offices and honors which they might have to bestow upon their partizans (if they had any to give), compared to those great interests of the South,—her safety, her honor, her thousands of millions of property, which are all in imminent peril, in which every Southern man has so vital a concern. According to every principle of enlightened reason, every patriotic Southern man may now expect that the old, and past, and worthless issues will be ignored :—that the Bell man, and the Breckinridge man, and the Douglas man will, now that their favorite candidates are off the stage, cease their party divisions, and all unite in forming a great Southern party in defence of their Southern homes ; in opposition to that great Northern party of Black Republicans who are banded together for our overthrow. Surely there are weighty interests enough, in *common*, to induce every Southern man not absolutely insane to forego and forget his bickerings with his neighbor, and joining with him, in heart and hand, and every faculty, lay their united offerings on the altar of the South. The result of this Presidential election will determine that there can be in future but two great parties in the United States—the Northern Abolition party, to overthrow the South, and the Southern anti-Abolition party, to protect the South from these inroads. Upon the triumph of Black Republicanism, in the person of Lincoln, there can be, consistently with our safety, but one party at the South. Democratic, Whig, Union, American, Douglas, Bell, Breckinridge, will all cease to be parties having any sensible meaning. They will be regarded as fossils of a past age, and will be swept off the field to make room for the one great Southern party which must now be organized to save the South. Let every patriotic man, then, in the South take his position in this party, and whether as Douglas, Bell or Breckinridge man, labor in behalf of the redemption of the South. If there be one, or a dozen, or perchance a thousand, scattered among these broken up parties, who are found still stupidly growling over their party grudges and refusing to lend their aid in rescuing their native South, let their late party associates leave them in their morbid selfishness, and all unite and work together in this our great Southern anti-Abolition party.

Alas ! "The Unionist."

If the Unionist, with all the evidence before him of the hostile designs of the Abolitionists, and the extreme dangers now hanging over the South, nevertheless refuses to aid, or, perhaps, even opposes the movement, let this great Southern party, with its true and earnest men, move on, without him, and save the South, in spite of him, for him and *his* family, as well as for themselves. In this great turning point in the destiny of the South no man can remain neutral. The aid of every loyal son is now needed to defend the rights and honor of his political mother, where nestles the home of his wife and children, and where is deposited all his property for their support. He who is not for her, in this hour of her extremity, is, without being conscious of it perhaps, against her, to the last end of her existence. Knowing, as he ought to know, the extreme dangers which are about to fall upon his country, THE "UNIONIST" OF THE SOUTH IN 1860, is the "SUBMISSIONIST," NOW, AND EVER WILL BE, HENCEFORTH AND FOREVER; AND WILL BE AN ABOLITIONIST OF THE NORTH IN 1870! To the honest but misguided "Unionist" (and not to those of that name who are conscious and premeditated traitors already to the South), this judgment may appear harsh and opprobrious. And in the unfeigned resentment which may spring up out of his present honest *intentions*, he may exclaim with Hazael of old, "But what! is thy servant a dog that he should do this great thing?"

But men do not know themselves, nor of what they are made; nor what they will do, under the force of circumstances. This man, who broke forth in this virtuous expression of earnest deprecation, may have been seen, "on the morrow," standing by the bedside of a confiding master, whom, in his feebleness and sickness, he had just smothered to death!— and a short time after, fulfilling, upon a defenceless people—their innocent little ones, and their feeble mothers—the very atrocities which had been foretold by the prophet, and which make the heart shudder to think of.

Ominous condition of the South!—and of the part which the "Southern Unionist" is enacting! He plays now into the hands of a hostile government, by his *submission*; and will be found, in the end, *acting* with the Northern Abolitionists, and aiding them in bringing down upon his country and his neighbors calamities which his soul now loaths at. In the one brief sentence in which the character of the "Southern Unionist" is just delineated, he may read, not a prediction (which implies uncertainty) of what he is to be, but the record which faithful history has already got her pen in hand, and is about to register concerning him.

THE VAIN REGRETS OF THE "SOUTHERN UNIONIST."

Who, alas! will be able to comprehend the feelings of remorse which will take possession of such a man (I mean the *honest* but *misguided* "Southern Unionist," and not the conscious traitor who marches under that flag), when, at some future period, he looks back upon the issues of 1860, and realizes the condition to which his country has been brought through his agency, supposing that his policy should prevail over the South! How humiliating will be the confessions which his honest candor will compel him to record against himself!

THE SOUL-CONFESSIONS OF THE "SOUTHERN UNIONIST" IN 1870.

"I was," he may say, "earnestly importuned in 1860 by my friends and my neighbors, to join with them in delivering the South from the heavy calamities which they saw impending over her, from the Black Republican rule which was to come over them by the election of Mr. Lincoln. They entreated and they urged me, by every motive which could be addressed to an intelligent mind—by duty, by patriotism, by honor, by interest, by the love which I bore for my wife and children, by the regard I had for their safety, and the sanctity of my home, to strike *then* and *without delay*, and *boldly*, for our rights, before our enemies should take possession of the government, and with the treasury, the army, and the navy, which they would then have at command to obtain such fearful

odds against us. But their entreaties and their arguments were in vain.
I was *timid*. I was *afraid* the General Government would coerce the
State, that it might bring on a "collision of arms," perhaps "civil war,"
and that if my State should secede alone, that Georgia, or South Carolina,
or Alabama, or North Carolina, would meanly take advantage of our diffi-
culties, and basely entice away our commerce, and ruin our trade, whilst
we were fighting in the common cause of the South. I was *afraid* that
in this commotion my business might be interrupted : I might not be able
to plant as much cotton, or sell as many goods, nor make as much money,
nor show off at Saratoga the next year and pass among the Northern snobs
as some great "wealthy Southerner," who had gone there to show them
how willing he was to be fed upon by every Northern blood-sucker. I did
not wish to have my *ease at home* interfered with, nor my *luxuries* curtailed ; and although I was willing to spend thousands to "show off" among
the snobs, and submitted, with the lavish grace, befitting a "wealthy
Southern gentleman," to the enormous exactions of landlords and trades-
men, and every body and thing else, at the North, with which I came in
contact ; and although I squandered my money profusely, to show the
"liberality of the Southerner,"—yet I was unwilling, when I returned to
my Southern home, to pay a dime to the State, in way of taxes, to defend
her liberties or protect my family or property. I *opposed* every effort at
resistance, although that resistance was urged on by very many of our best
citizens, and for causes which I could not but regard as having very great
weight. I could not distrust their judgment because in everything else
they had my confidence ; nor could I doubt their sincerity, because they
were willing to trust their all upon the issue. But their resistance, it was
plain to me, would lead to "disunion" ; to the breaking up of this "great
government at Washington," and the "dissolution of our glorious Union."
And as I had always belonged to the "Union" party, and as a Unionist
who should always oppose the Disunionist, I opposed these Resistance
men, eminent in wisdom and sincere in their designs, as I believe them to
be. I tried to persuade myself (and at least succeeded), that the dangers
to the South were not *so* great and imminent as the Resistance men made
them out to be ; and with the aid of the Yankees in the community, I
succeeded in persuading every timid and indolent man (ever too ready to
grasp at any excuse for submission), that resistance might be *postponed*
for a time ; that we should "try Mr. Lincoln"; wait for him to "commit
some overt act" ; that the "Black Republicans would not do what they
had threatened" ; and that there was a great "conservative party at the
North," who were going to do great things for us, and put down the Abolitionists. By these persuasions, I succeeded in gathering together a
strong anti-Resistance party, and tied the South down to submission.

"But I must here say, in these the secret confessions of my soul, that
I never went to the polls to cast my vote as a member of this "Union"
party, without having my sensibilities as a Southern man painfully dis-
turbed. There, on the one hand, were to be seen the earnest Resistance
men urging on the people, by appeals to the noblest principles of their
nature, courageously to come forward and vindicate the honor and rights
of their native South, by *resisting* our enemies: whilst on the other side
were to be seen herded together among the 'Union men,' the selfish, the
craven, and the indolent, mixed up with every Yankee adventurer who
had left his Northern Abolition home to sojourn here for a short time,
'doing business'—each, encouraging the other, to *submit* to our enemies,
by appealing to the most sordid motives of fear, and money-making. It

was with much humiliating misgiving, whether I was in the right place for a Southern man, when I found myself at all elections in close association with these Northern men—having no harmony of feeling with the South—no permanent home, or fixed property amongst us, and claiming to be citizens of distant and hostile communities. But if these were my *party associates;* to whom, was I opposing myself? To the natives of the soil, who had the deepest interests at stake—to my near neighbors, and most cherished friends, in whose wisdom and integrity I had every confidence.''

" But I yielded myself up to the principles of Unionism. I and my party *opposed resistance;* we preached and *encouraged submission;* and our counsels prevailed; and now, at the end of ten years, I look around me, and find these to be fruits of my work:

" The South is fettered, spiritless, reduced to poverty and imbecility; whilst the North has fattened by her submission; has become rich and powerful, and is raging with the fierce spirit of abolition aggression. My counsels, alas! have become fatal to her. She has *submitted* too long: she is now, indeed, too feeble to resist; I realize now, for the first time, the stunning import of the words :—I SUBMIT TO THE EMANCIPATION OF MY SLAVES.''

Such, resistance men of the South, must be the unhappy reflections, not of the "Southern Unionist" merely, but of every man, no matter under what name, or party banner, he may act, who opposes prompt, vigorous, decided action against the hostile rule of the Black Republicans. Disguise it as he may, to deceive his conscience, *postponement* of effectual resistance *now,* to some future period of "overt acts" of further aggression, is *submission, now;—submission forever!* If these Procrastinators do not see, in the FACT which, like some tall giant, stalks abroad before their eyes, *to wit: that we are soon to be ruled over by our deadliest enemies,*—enough of motive, to throw off that government, and rule ourselves,—then it must be because they would think it preferable to wait for the "overt act" of being well kicked and trodden under foot,—before they took any measures to prevent it; although they had been threatened with these indignities by certain associated bullies who had both the ample power and the thorough good will to fulfil their threats.

EVERYTHING TO BE LOST BY POSTPONEMENT: NOTHING TO BE GAINED BY IT.

And if, with all the favorable circumstances in which we now find ourselves, which an overruling Providence seems to have brought together especially to aid us, and which we may never expect again to concur in our future history,—these "procrastinators" are too *timid* to strike for their country, and *shrink now* from the danger, what may we expect from them in future, when, our enemies having got possession of the Government, with all its mighty engines of oppression, shall riot in their strength; and when we, with each day of our subjection (or rather subjugation) to them, shall become weaker and less able to resist? If *fears* unman them now, when is *manhood* and *courage* to take their place? If ever, when? and under what possible conjuncture of circumstances? Let them tell us, or cease to delude us with ghostly hopes, to which they can assign neither "local habitation or a name."

Let every true man, then, of every party in the South, ruminate well this question. Let him examine it on this side and that, above and below, and all around, and see whether *postponement* of resistance now is not submission now—*submission forever*—with all its disastrous consequences. If no other conclusion but this can be arrived at, then *procrastination* is *ruin;* and with this conviction the resistance party will find its ranks soon thronged with most valuable allies; for the procrastinator is not a submissionist from principle, but only by mistake.

That the destiny of the South is to be decided by the craven *submissionist*, is a verdict which would carry dismay to every Southern household, and would blister with endless shame the manhood of her sons. That she should *submit, without a struggle,* to have all her priceless advantages taken away from her, (which is the counsel of the submissionist), at the demand of her insulting enemies, is a thought which is not to be tolerated. How utterly demoralized must that people be, who, when everything that is dear to them on earth is at stake, *shrink back* from its defence, from the most ignominious of all motives, the fear of danger and of mere animal sloth! That the South should servilely bend her neck to her enemies, and submit to have her millions of slaves emancipated, her thousands of millions of property taken away from her, her citizens reduced to poverty and want, a servile and debased race elevated to an equality with her citizens, and their families degraded by such an intercourse—and that she should submit to all this, with the utmost loathing, merely because she was too *cowardly,* and too *indolent,* and too *selfish,* to make the proper sacrifices to protect herself, is to suppose an intensity of baseness on her part which would consign her to everlasting infamy. History would be unable to find words to record the hissing scorn which such pusillanimity would deserve. And yet such is the despicable condition to which the *submissionist* would reduce her.

I call upon you then, *men* of the South, (not the poltroons of the South) *true men* of the South, (not traitors of the South), to rally to the rescue of your cherished, native land. Suffer not the counsels of the submissionist to prevail. Honor and duty call upon you for resistance,—*undying resistance,*—to defend your country against the ready purposes of her enemies. And never before have honor and duty been more surely the path of true wisdom, leading to permanent safety. Falter not then, either as individual, or State, because your neighbor may, perchance, be a submissionist; but go on without him, and leave him to his infamy. The honor of neither State, nor man, is in the keeping of his neighbor. Each must protect his own, and leave to impartial history to record how manfully he has guarded it. What would it avail to South Carolina if Georgia, or any other Southern State, acting under the noble impulses of a manly courage, should throw down the gauntlet of defiance to her enemies, and declare before the world that a Black Republican government should not rule over her citizens,—what would it avail, I say, to South Carolina in rescuing her name from the contempt of mankind, and the execration of her own children, if she were found submitting to the degrading bondage! Would the gallantry of her Southern sister atone for the infamy she will have brought upon herself; or sponge from the record the "dastard" and "poltroon" which history will have written against her name!

Let each man (and each State) then act out for himself according to the impulses of his own high duty and honor, and without being influenced by the pusillanimity of his neighbor. And as the cause of the South is common to all, and as the interests at stake are too stupendous to be given up without ruin to each—we may rest assured that when the day of decisive action shall arrive, they will be found all moving in concert, without any previous agreement having been formed, pledging them to that purpose. Among the States thus moving on earnestly for their deliverance, I think, gentlemen, you know what place South Carolina will occupy in the picture.

APPENDIX.

A.

People at the North, where the movements of the Abolitionists are duly chronicled in the daily prints, are fully aware of these hostile purposes, and contemplate with amazement the doltish sloth and apathy which pervade the South, whilst their deadly enemies are industriously sapping and mining under their very *citadel*, and will be soon ready to blow it up into fragments. What we fail to see, is plainly manifest to them; and among the few who are there not under the sway of abolitionism, and have given expression to their thoughts in a public form, there are some, (such as Mr. O'Connor, Mr. Cushing and Mr. Barnard,) seeing, as they do, the awful calamities which these schemes of the abolitionists will entail upon the South, who express the opinion that the South, as a matter of course, will not, and cannot, submit to such a government without utter ruin and dishonor. Nor do I think the South would submit, even for an hour, if they were properly informed of the designs of the party which will soon, with Mr. Lincoln at its head, have the control of the government. From prudential considerations, which, however, I think they have carried to a mistaken extreme, the newspapers of the South have failed to keep their readers informed of these dangerous measures; and facts, which they who are most deeply interested in knowing but are yet ignorant of, are known only to those at a distance, who have but little concern in the matter. What Southern man, whether the owner or not the owner of slaves, would consent to live under the government of Abolitionists, when he knew that the settled purpose of that government was the emancipation of all the slaves, and making the slave (the inferior race) equal to the white man. The poorest white man in the South (except he be already utterly debased by his vices or his crimes,) would spurn such a thought, and would rise up with indignation against a government who would thus attempt to degrade him and his family to the level of the Negro. And yet such is the undoubted, indisputable design of the Black Republican party when they shall take possession of the government and have power over the South. In proof of this, fact might be piled upon fact, until the most incredulous would be satisfied. These proofs will not here be repeated; but if any be desirous of satisfying himself on this point, he will find the facts accumulated (a few only out of many more which might have been added) in one of the Notes to a pamphlet lately published in Charleston, entitled "The South Alone should Govern the South, and African Slavery should be Controlled by those only who are Friendly to it."

D3

 34

B.

Some months before the Abolition raid in Virginia, old John Brown, H. Kagi, and others, had put forth at the North a "Plan for the Abolition of Slavery," for the purpose, as they stated, of "forming Associations throughout the country of all persons who are willing to pledge themselves publicly to favor the enterprise, and render support and assistance of any kind." The late insurrection in Texas was a development of this *improved* scheme of diabolical ingenuity, as well as an exemplification of the *intense hatred* which is cherished by the Abolitionist against the *Southern slaveholder*. This "Plan," as well as the "Plan of the Abolitionists for *secret circulation*," may be found also in a Note to the pamphlet just referred to, ("The South Alone should Govern the South;") and by comparing the occurrences in Texas, until the plot was discovered and arrested, with these plans concocted by John Brown, we will be at no loss to understand the mode in which the Giddings and Garrisonian wing of the party intend, in future, to carry on this warfare. The following letters from Texas are taken from the New York *Day Book* of September 8th, and give information as to the manner in which the Abolition plot was conducted there, which should operate as a warning to us to be vigilant and resolute:

THE ABOLITION PLOT IN TEXAS.

IMPORTANT LETTER FROM JUDGE REAGAN.—INJURY TO NEW YORK MERCHANTS.

Hon. John H. Reagan, M. C., has written a letter to his brother Morris Reagan, which is published in the Austin *Gazette*. Here is the letter:—

PALESTINE, Aug. 18, 1860.

Dear Brother: I was called to the court-house yesterday, when writing to you, to attend a meeting in relation to the negro disturbances, and did not write to you what is going on in that respect.

A plot has been discovered in Tennessee colony, and extending out from there, between some white men and negros, similar to that in Dallas, Ellis and Tarrant counties. Indeed, it is regarded as a part of the same plot—to poison as many people as they could on Sunday night before the election, and on the day of the election to burn the houses and kill as many of the women and children as they could while the men were gone to the election, and then kill the men as they returned home.

On last Sunday two white men, who lived up near Catfish Bayou, were hung as the ringleaders of the plot in this county. Our vigilance committees and patrol have been active here in guarding against other dangers and in investigating this matter.

One negro has been hung in Henderson and one in Cherokee county, and we are informed that the town of Henderson has been burned—supposed by incendiaries—but no particulars yet.

I am strongly persuaded, from all I can learn, that these things must be the result of an abolition plot arranged elsewhere than in Texas, and that its execution has been committed to the desperate set of Kansas outlaws or similar men. And I do not think one of them ought to be permitted to leave the State alive where his complicity can be clearly shown.

Your brother, JOHN H. REAGAN.

The New Orleans *Picayune* says *that the burning of towns in Texas will fall heavily upon New York merchants, they having enjoyed the greater part of the trade of the State.*

THE ABOLITION RAID IN TEXAS.

[From a Special Correspondent.]

FORT WORTH, Texas, Aug. 12, 1860.

By the last mail the Secretary forwarded you a copy of the proceedings of perhaps one of the largest meetings ever assembled together on a similar occasion in northern Texas. I propose to give you a short history of the past few weeks, the state of public sentiment, as far as I have been able to appreciate it, (the feelings of those present are portrayed in the fourth and fifth resolutions sent you,) and to make a few observations on the state of parties here, the necessary consequences which must follow the election of Lincoln to the presidency.

About five weeks ago the town of Dallas was burned; on the same day Denton shared the same fate, and several other towns in northern Texas were fired. In quick succession there were a number of country residences set on fire. Quite a number of our citizens had all they had on earth burnt up—wheat, corn, rye, oats, fencing, &c., &c. A few weeks before these things occurred, a fire had been discovered about 12, M., in the store of Messrs. Field and Kennedy, of this place. These circumstances led to the formation of Vigilance Committees in almost every county in northern Texas. In the county of Dallas the discovery was made that the negros had fired the town of Dallas and the residences and farms of its citizens; that there was in each county a leader who was a white man, whose name was kept secret from most of the negros, and that slow matches were furnished by him to the negros, which they applied to the houses which they determined to destroy. There was also found a large quantity of poison in the possession of the negros, which, when gathered together, would have filled a half barrel. It was also discovered that these Abolition incendiaries had been sent here by Abolition Aid Societies. In Fort Worth, a suspicious character, recently from the State of Minnesota, was carefully watched. He was betrayed by one of the negros, detected, and hung without an hour's warning. He had told that he expected a large number of six shooters on every day, and since he was hung, *the revolvers, three hundred in number, have come to his address, marked "clocks,"* in three separate boxes, one hundred in each. These discoveries are not confined to Dallas and Tarrant counties, but extend to a very considerable portion of northern Texas. The 1st Monday in August (election day,) was the day of general revolt. I will add that the man hung in Fort Worth was not the only one who shared the same fate, and there has been a general stampede among the suspicious, several of whom could only save their necks by flight. The Vigilant Committees have determined to order no one to leave, but to hang every man who puts his feet on Texas soil, avowing the *"doctrines"* of the Free Soil party. To appreciate the feelings of our citizens, you would have to be in our midst at this time. Our houses, &c., were not only to be burned and our citizens murdered, but *the young women* and *little girls* were *to be saved to become the wives or concubines of these fiends of hell.*

Our citizens look upon a Free-soiler alone, as a murderer and incendiary—as one who advocates principles which must necessarily lead to every species of iniquity known in the catalogue of crime. They know their is an Abolition Aid Society forwarding six shooters here with which to murder us, and then commit *every species of enormity on the mothers, sisters, wives and daughters of southern citizens.* The scene is too revolting to contemplate. I would to God it was untrue. And be not surprised when I tell you that we will *hang* every man who does not live above suspicion. Necessity now reverses the rule, for it is better for us to hang ninety-nine innocent (suspicious) men than to let one guilty one pass, for the guilty one endangers the peace of society, and every man coming from a northern State should live above suspicion. Such is the universal sentiment of this community, and soon must and will be of the entire South.

The great heart of the people here is with Breckinridge and Lane. They look upon Douglas' "Popular Sovereignty" doctrine as "Free Soil" in tendency and practice, and consequently destructive of the rights of the South, incendiary in practice if not in principle. They believe that Lincoln is the head and representative of this *Abolition Aid Society,* which sent John Brown to Virginia, and which is now giving us so much trouble here; and I believe I am not in the dark when I say that if Lincoln is elected, it will take five hundred thousand troops to inaugurate him President of the United States. To believe that the South would submit to it, with the train of calamities which must of necessity follow, is to believe that we are paltroons, and destitute of every sentimental patriotism. The history of every revolution which has occurred on earth, shows that it never was left to a popular vote; but outraged humanity commenced resistance, as our forefathers did at Boston, and a whole people rushed to their relief. We desire to preserve the Union, but we want a Union of free, equal and sovereign States, with that protection which the Constitution guaranties to us; just such a Union as is represented by the party which nominated Breckinridge and Lane, and in no other way can this Union be saved.

Yours, respectfully, J. W. S.

FURTHER ACCOUNTS OF THE ABOLITION RAID.

[From an Old Correspondent.]

MARSHALL, TEXAS, Aug. 12, 1860.

Editors of the Evening Day Book:

The wildest excitement prevails throughout the north-western, north-eastern, and the central portions of Texas, in consequence of *Abolition incendiarism.* I have no doubt but you have seen, ere this reaches you, the burning of Dallas, Denton, Black Jack Grove, and quite a large number of stores and mills. Loss estimated at between $1,500,000 and $2,000,000. Since then the *Abolitionists* have been detected in attempts to fire a number of other towns South of the above, and in an extensive plan of insurrection among the negros, headed by these demons of hell. On some plantations the negros have been examined, and arms and ammunition in considerable amount have been found in their possession; they all admit they were given to them by these *Lincolnites*. Every day we hear of the burning of some town, mill, store, or farmhouse. Henderson was burnt to ashes on the 6th instant, being the general election day for State and county officers. We hear of two or three other towns burnt on the same day. *Women and children* have been so frightened by these burnings and threatened rebellion of the negros, that in several instances they have *left their homes in their fright, and when found were almost confirmed maniacs!* Military companies are organized all over the State, and one-half of our citizens do constant patrol duty. But unfortunately up to this time Judge Lynch has had the honor to preside only in ten cases of whites, (northern Lincolnites) and about sixty-five of negros, all of whom were hung or burnt, as to the degree of their implication in the rebellion and burning. The plan was to burn all of the towns, thereby destroy the arms and ammunition, also country stores, mills, farms and corn cribs, &c. Then on election day they were to be headed by John Browns, and march South for Houston and Galveston city, where they would all unite, and after pillaging and burning those two cities, the negros were promised by these devils incarnate, that they would have in readiness a number of vessels, and would take them forthwith to Mexico, where they would be free. The *credulity of the negro* is so great, that he can be *induced to believe almost anything,* no matter how impossible it may be, particularly when he is informed by a shrewd white man that the thing can be done, and that he will lead them on and accomplish the object. But the end is not yet. I believe that the northern churches are at the bottom of this whole affair—in fact the fanatics have already acknowledged it. They say that this Texas raid is in revenge for the expulsion of some of their brethren of the Methodist church from Texas, about twelve or eighteen months ago, for preaching and teaching Abolition incendiarism to the negros in northern Texas. Unless the churches send out new recruits of John Browns, I fear the boys will have nothing to do this winter, (as they have hung all that can be found,) the school boys have become so excited by the sport in hanging Abolitionists, that the schools are completely deserted, they having formed companies, and will go seventy-five or one hundred miles on horseback to participate in a single execution of the sentence of Judge Lynch's Court. It has now become a settled conviction in the South *that this Union cannot subsist one day after Abe Lincoln has been declared President,* if God, in his infinite wisdom, should permit him to live that long; for they, (the people of the South) have made up their minds that they had rather die, sword in hand, in defence of their homes, their wives, their children and slaves, in defence of the Constitution, the laws, and their sacred honor, than *tamely submit to an organized system of robbery, a degraded and loathsome scheme of amalgamation,* a breaking up of the compromises of the Constitution, and a total exclusion of the South from the common Territories of the country won by their blood and treasure.

W. R. D. W.

Citizens of the South, do not delude yourselves with the opinion that none of these emissaries have crawled in among you, and are even now lurking within your respective States. The spear of an Ithurial would start up many from their present disguises. Alabama and Georgia, and more recently, Virginia and North Carolina, and South Carolina, have been polluted by their presence, and have been compelled, for their crimes, to help them to the cheap martyrdom which they sought.

And now,

Husbands,

Fathers,

Brothers,

reperuse certain sentences in those letters, which, from the horror which they inspire, deserve the emphasis with which they are distinguished. Ponder the unutterable degradation which is there designed for you, and then say, what union can we have with a people who can devise such enormities, and what perils and sacrifices should we not rather endure than submit to the government of a party which encourages, promotes, and presses on such outrages!

C.

From the beginning of the war in Kansas, arising out of the attempt of the Northern Abolitionists to drive out the Southern Slaveholder from that territory, the writer of this, became profoundly impressed with the importance to the South of getting possession of it. From its geographical position, he considered that it was worth thousands of millions of dollars to the South, as a fortress which would guard all the territories laying back of it; from Missouri on the North, to Texas on the South; all which would ultimately become Slave States, if the barrier of Kansas were not broken down. The possession of all those States then, being dependent upon the possession of Kansas, he considered that no *ordinary* efforts should be made by the South, to secure Kansas, as a State favorable to our institutions. The abolitionist North, with that far-seeing sagacity which they always exercise when their *interests* are at stake, immediately organized societies to aid "Emigrants" in going to Kansas and occupying it; and with great energy and liberality provided large funds to accomplish their purpose. The South was appealed to, for the purpose of furnishing aid, also, to her emigrants. The writer was applied to, by the Kansas Association of Charleston, composed of some of our most distinguished and public spirited citizens; and in March, 1856, nearly four years before the article of "Python" was published in De Bow's Review, he addressed a letter to Wm. Whaley, Esq., the Chairman of the Executive Committee of that Association; in which (whilst he asked the privilege of joining them in their contributions) he expressed his views somewhat fully, upon the very great importance to the South of the issue then made in Kansas.

In allusion to the extraordinary efforts which were made by the abolition "Emigrant Aid Societies," to send men and money into Kansas to abolitionize and take it from the South, he urged corresponding exertions to be made to save that territory, as rightfully belonging to us, and as being worthy of very great sacrifices to be made, for its possession. Without having followed out the disastrous consequences, to which the *loss* of Kansas would legitimately and inevitably lead, as "Python" has done, the writer contented himself with merely pointing out the *immediate* effects; which he thought were quite sufficient to wake up every Southern man of ordinary forethought to exert himself to save that territory to us. He spoke of Kansas, "as the 'Malakoff' fortress, the taking of which, would decide our victory, in this battle with abolitionism in that quarter of our Republic;—a battle, in which from three to five States, were the prizes, to be won or lost, to the South, and her cherished institutions."

But the writer laments to say, that, like "Python," he "wrote and spoke in vain." The citizens of the South could not be induced as at present to look at, and provide against a danger which appeared so remote. They were slumbering and idle, whilst their enemies were actively at work : and whilst the Abolitionists contributed their hundreds of thousands of dollars to equip and send out, and colonize their emigrants in Kansas—a few scanty thousands only, were all that were parsimoniously doled out by the whole South; which was utterly inadequate, to encourage any emigrants to leave their homes, or to aid the few who went there. The "pennywise," chuckled over the cunning, by which he escaped making his contribution to the common cause; and the meanness of his avarice which saved him a few dimes has been rewarded, by the loss of a territory which, judged by the consequences which will flow from it, is worth thousands of millions of dollars, and will result in the "constitutional" emancipation of his slaves!

It is but justice however to say, that Kansas was left unaided by the South, not so much from penuriousness, as from the *poverty* of the great bulk of our people. The whole course of Federal legislation has tended to divert money from the South ;—which leaves her scanty of funds for any public-spirited purpose ;—and for the same reason has accumulated abundant capital at the North and in the abolition States; which enables that section to subscribe largely for any scheme of public policy—even if it be, to hire the loafers of their cities, to drive the slave-holder from the common territories.

Thus does our *union* with them, cut us both ways, like a two-edged sword. We are first impoverished, by Federal laws which make them rich and powerful, and us feeble and poor; and then they use that very power and riches, of which we have been drained by them, to swoop down upon us, farther to rob and oppress us.

CONSTITUTION OF 1860 ASSOCIATION.

I.—The members whose names are hereto subscribed, constitute themselves an Association, for the purpose of promoting resistance, by the slaveholding States, to the aggressions of the non-slaveholding States.

II.—The Association shall have a President, to be selected by a majority of the members present, and a Recording Secretary, to be appointed by the President.

III.—There shall be appointed, by the President, an Executive Committee, to consist of fifteen members, to whom shall be entrusted such duties for promoting the objects of the Association, as shall, in its discretion be necessary, with power to appoint under it a Committee of Publication, and such other committees as it may deem proper.

IV.—Upon subscribing these articles, each member shall pay the sum of five dollars to the Treasurer, who shall be appointed by the Executive Committee.

V.—The Association shall be convened whenever in the opinion of the President, or of the Executive Committee, it shall be deemed requisite.

The Secretary and Treasurer of the 1860 Association is Mr. WM. TENNENT, JR., No. 6 Broad Street, Charleston.